Probate Made Simple

How to Save Time, Ensure Family Harmony, and Reduce Stress

Paul Deloughery, Esq.

Probate Made Simple

Independently Published

Copyright © 2024, Paul Deloughery, Esq.

Published in the United States of America

231027-02417.4.1

ISBN: 9798883995650

For more information on 90-Minute Books, including finding out how you
can publish your own book, visit 90minutebooks.com or call (863) 318-0464

Here's What's Inside...

Introduction

As a probate lawyer with more than 25 years of experience, I have seen firsthand how confusing and stressful the probate process can be. Many families spend years tangled up in complex legal procedures, not knowing how to properly handle their loved one's estate. I have also witnessed bitter family feuds erupt over disputes about the will and distribution of assets.

This heartbreaking family discord is often an unintended consequence of a probate process that was not managed correctly.

There is a better way. My mission in writing this book is to provide clear, step-by-step guidance on how to navigate probate efficiently and minimize the burden on you and your family. This book will help demystify the probate process and legal terminology so you can understand exactly what needs to be done at each stage. With the practical tips and step-by-step guidance provided, you will be equipped to navigate through the probate process more efficiently, potentially reducing both the time and cost typically associated with it.

You will learn how to locate the decedent's accounts and assets, value assets, pay off debts, and distribute inheritances while avoiding expenses and aggravation. I will help you work smoothly with the court, heirs, and other attorneys to settle the estate by the book. You will also find best practices for communicating tactfully with family members to maintain harmony now and in the future.

Whether you need to probate a large multi-million-dollar estate or simply transfer the deceased's home and bank accounts, this book will empower you to handle the process with competence and ease. My proven methods will ensure probate does not become a long, costly headache for you or cause lasting rifts between your loved ones. Let's get started demystifying probate so you can grieve, heal, and secure your family's legacy.

Simplifying Probate,

Paul

PROBATE ASSETS:

These are assets that are owned solely by the deceased person at the time of their death, and which do not pass to others through designations such as beneficiary designations or joint ownership. Examples include real estate owned solely in the deceased person's name, personal property, bank accounts held solely in the deceased person's name, and vehicles registered in the deceased person's name.

PROBATE VS. NON-PROBATE ASSETS

NON-PROBATE ASSETS:

These are assets that pass to other individuals upon the owner's death, without having to go through probate. Examples include life insurance policies with named beneficiaries, retirement accounts with designated beneficiaries, properties held jointly with right of survivorship, and assets in a trust.

Chapter One
Figure Out If You Need Probate and What Kind

Probate is a court process that helps administer a deceased person's assets when they die. It is a way to ensure that things get distributed to the right people, whether that be creditors or beneficiaries and so on. The important thing to know is that some things go through the court process, and some do not.

Step one is to identify the non-probate assets. Those are assets that automatically transfer to a beneficiary upon death, so they bypass the probate process. Examples include life insurance policies with a named beneficiary, retirement accounts like IRAs and 401(k)s with a named beneficiary, jointly owned property with right of survivorship, and assets held in a trust.

Now that you know what is not a probate asset, anything else is a probate asset. That would include solely owned property, meaning property that is in the deceased person's name alone. It might also include individual bank accounts without a payable-on-death beneficiary. It also includes personal belongings. Antique furniture, artwork and investments without a designated beneficiary are also typically probate assets.

In probate, those assets are distributed according to the will, if there is one, or according to state law, if there is not a will. Again, the key difference lies in how assets are titled and whether they have a designated beneficiary.

What Is Small Estate Administration?

Another exception to having to do probate is if the assets owned by the deceased person are less than a certain value. In Arizona, an estate can be processed as a small estate if the total value of personal property is under $75,000 and real property is under $100,000. That value can be determined by deducting liens and encumbrances. In other words, if you have a $500,000 house, but there is a $450,000 mortgage on it, then there is only $50,000 of equity. That is under $100,000, so that qualifies as a small estate. Personal property, for example, includes things like bank accounts and vehicles. If those are under $75,000, that also qualifies as a small estate.

You also need to meet certain conditions. For personal property to qualify as a small estate, at least 30 days must have passed since the deceased person's death. For personal property, an affidavit can be used to claim assets if there is no pending petition for a personal representative or if it has been over a year since the personal representative was discharged. That was all for personal property. For real property, it is similar, but you have to wait six months after death. You must ensure that all funeral expenses, last illness expenses, and unsecured debts are paid. The Small Estate Administration can certainly save time and reduce legal complexities for some situations as long as they qualify. It is a good thing to at least keep in mind.

Hunting for a Will

If you do not know whether the deceased person had a will, you end up going on a little bit of a scavenger hunt. You can start by checking with the deceased person's attorney. They may have an original will, or at least, they might have a copy of the will. You can also search the deceased person's personal documents and safe deposit boxes. Additionally, you can ask family members who might know the whereabouts of the will. In some states, but not in Arizona, wills are public record. A person can file their will with the local probate court before they have died. However, in Arizona, that is not the way it works.

Another thing is to look around for a probate binder. When a person goes to an attorney, they will get a fancy portfolio that is usually green, blue, or red. It looks nice, and it says, "Estate Planning Portfolio" or something like that on the spine. In it, you should find all the estate plan documents, like powers of attorney and living will and other things. Hopefully, there would also be the will inside that.

What Does Waive Bond Mean?

The next issue is figuring out if a bond is needed. A bond is a type of insurance that protects the estate from mishandling by a personal representative, but it can be expensive. That's why a will usually will specifically waive this requirement. You will need to read the will and see if it mentions waiving the bond requirement for the personal representative. If it does, the personal representative can serve without buying a bond. Again, that simplifies the process and saves expenses. If the bond is not waived, the personal representative will need to get a bond or somehow ensure that the estate assets are protected.

A bond can be kind of expensive. For a large estate, if it is millions of dollars, it can be expensive. It might be cheaper to restrict some of the accounts or restrict real estate and only post a bond for a certain amount. The problem with that is, it means the personal representative cannot do anything with those things without a court order. That then requires going to court and having a hearing, which raises expenses.

There are options, but if the bond is not waived, those options can be complicated and expensive.

Holographic Wills

A holographic will is one that is handwritten. It doesn't need to say "Will" on it. It merely requires that the signature and the material provisions are in the handwriting of the deceased person. Let me share two stories about handwritten wills because it is not always clear what qualifies. These are two actual situations in which something that you would never think was a will turned out to be a will.

About 20 years ago, my law firm represented the natural children of a father who passed away. The father was remarried, so a stepmother was involved. The father liked drinking alcohol. One time, when he was inebriated, he wrote a grocery list to his wife, and it said something like, "Eggs, milk, bread. You get the ranch when I die." Then he signed and dated it.

That ranch was land used to raise horses in Arizona and was worth about $5 million. After going all the way to trial, the jury determined that that qualified as a will. The stepmom got everything. Dad should have been more careful about what he wrote when he was drinking.

Recently, we have been dealing with a very similar situation. It involves a Christmas card. This Christmas card says something like, "Merry Christmas, I love you. Remember, you get the house." Again, it was signed and dated. We are probating a Christmas card. It was kind of interesting. I wanted to make sure this got special treatment when filing it with the court, so I took it with me to court. You should have seen the probate clerk's eyes when I gave her a Christmas card. She thought I was being nice to her because this happened in mid-December. But I said, "No, that is the will."

My Concern for You

A lot of people do not understand when probate is needed or if it is not needed. For example, if they see that their loved one had a trust, they assume there is no probate needed. However, you also have to look and see if things were transferred to the trust. For example, if they had a trust but the house was in their personal name, a probate needs to be done.

Also, a lot of people kind of assume that if there is a will, then you have to go to probate, and that is not necessarily true. For example, if all the bank accounts have a payable-on-death beneficiary, and if the house is jointly owned with a surviving spouse, the will might be irrelevant because there are no probate assets that need to be processed through the probate court. There is no simple answer to that. You need to talk to an attorney to make sure one way or the other.

Essential Takeaway:
Assess the size and complexity of the estate.

If the estate qualifies as a small estate (under certain value thresholds), you may avoid formal probate. For larger or more complex estates, determine whether informal or formal probate is appropriate based on factors like the existence of a will, the nature of the assets, and potential disputes among heirs.

Chapter Two
Filing of Petition for Formal Probate or Application for Informal Probate

Informal Versus Formal?

Informal versus formal refers to who determines whether the will is valid and who appoints the personal representative. I should back up and explain that the personal representative is the Arizona word for executor. In some states, they say executor and in others, they might say administrator. In Arizona, the person who handles the deceased person's affairs after they have died, other than in a trust, is called the personal representative. That is who gets appointed by the court.

The difference between informal and formal is this. Informal is if certain criteria are met, then the process of going to probate is simpler. By simpler, I mean it gets handled administratively at the probate filing counter. Formal is something different. Formal is if it cannot be done informally or administratively, then it has to be done with special treatment. In that case, the determination of whether to admit the will and whether to appoint the personal representative gets handled by a judge or a probate commissioner. That is the difference between formal and informal.

How Do I Get Appointed as a Personal Representative?

First, figure out if there is a will or not, and then look in the will and see if you are nominated to be the personal representative. The will should say that. If you are first in line in the will, that will certainly make your job easier. It does not guarantee you are going to be appointed, but in all likelihood, you are going to be the one appointed.

If there is no will, then there is a certain priority of people who can be appointed. The surviving spouse has priority. Next in line is an adult child of the decedent. After that come the parents of the decedent, if they survive. After that, a brother or sister would be next in line, and so on. Determine if other people might be entitled to become the personal representative.

You might need to get those people to agree to you being appointed. If there is a will that nominates you, that certainly makes it easier.

After you have hopefully figured out that you are entitled to be appointed, and you have priority, then you file what is called an application with the court if it is informal. Again, that gets handled administratively. If it is formal, meaning that the probate filing counter or the clerk of court will not let you do it administratively, then you have to go the formal route. You do that with what is called a petition. These are two different things. They say essentially the same thing, but they have two different tracks. One is administrative, and the other ends up going in front of a probate judge.

What Forms and Documents Do I Need to File with the Court?

If it is being done informally, you file an application for probate of will if there is a will and for informal appointment of personal representatives. If it is being done formally, then it is a petition for probate of will and appointment of personal representative. Again, one is an application, and the other is a petition. They both do the same thing. Then, other things have to be filed with the court.

You have to sign an acceptance of appointment as the personal representative. There is a probate information form that asks for a lot of personal information, such as your eye color, your height, your weight, your hair color, your sex, and your social security number. The court requires that to know how to contact you because if you end up taking all the money and moving to Jamaica, the court wants to be able to track you down and figure out how to get the money back.

There is also some training you need to do in Arizona, and one is for non-licensed fiduciaries. It is general training about what it means to be a fiduciary and what your responsibilities are. You are held to a high standard, and you have to obey the law. There is further training for personal representatives, which goes through the basic requirements after you are appointed. For example, you have to prepare an inventory, send notice to the creditors, and know how to handle the creditors. You have to treat the heirs or the beneficiaries fairly. You have to file proof of having taken those two trainings with the court.

Assuming everything gets accepted, the court will issue what is called Letters of Personal Representative. I know that sounds funny. They are not sending you a letter. It is a one- or two-page piece of paper that is called Letters of Personal Representative. That is what gives you the official authority to handle bank accounts, sell real estate, deal with creditors, and more.

A Key Point to Remember

We always try to file things informally because it is a lot faster, but sometimes that does not work. Sometimes, the clerk of the court or probate registrar will not accept what we filed, so they ask us to go in front of a judge. For example, we recently had a situation in which we had an original will and a photocopy of a codicil. A codicil is an amendment. It was so crazy because the will just said everything went to the kids equally, and the amendment didn't change that. But we had to have a hearing, publish notice of the hearing and serve the three kids with notice of this hearing, all because we only had a photocopy of the amendment.

Frankly, it would have been easier if the loved one had ripped everything up before they died. Then, the estate would have gone under the statute, and that would have been a lot easier. However, because of the situation and the fact that we did not have an original of one document, we had to go in front of a judge and have a hearing. That delayed the process by about two months.

The good news is that most things are fixable through the court system. Unfortunately, it does delay things if you have to go in front of a judge.

Essential Takeaway:
Ensure accuracy and completeness when filing.

The petition/application should accurately reflect all pertinent details of the estate and comply with Arizona legal requirements. Avoid common pitfalls by double-checking the deceased's information, the list of heirs, and the asset details.

Chapter Three
Notification of Interested Parties

How Do You Find Beneficiaries, Heirs, and Creditors?

The personal representative needs to notify the heirs and beneficiaries listed in the will when the probate begins. There is a specific definition of heirs that is more complicated than I can go into in this book right now. A basic explanation is if there is a surviving spouse, then the spouse is an heir. If there are children of the deceased person and the surviving spouse, then the surviving spouse is still the only heir. If it was a second family or a blended family and the surviving children are not related to the surviving spouse, then both the children and surviving spouse are heirs. If there is no spouse and no children, then the parents or the parents' descendants are heirs and so on.

There is no simple answer for who an heir is, but the heirs are entitled to be notified. The people who are supposed to receive something in a will are also supposed to be notified.

Ultimately, after the personal representative is appointed, that person has to publish a notice to creditors. That is a notice that is published in a newspaper of general circulation in the county where the probate is being handled. It is not the newspaper that you pick up at the grocery store. This is more a kind of newspaper of legal notices.

I have only seen a physical copy of these kinds of newspapers maybe once or twice in my lifetime. The main purpose is to fulfill the legal duty. This was a requirement that was thought up probably 150 years ago when there was no internet and no social media. At the time, they thought putting something in the newspaper was the best way to advertise someone had died. Creditors need to come forward, so there is a publication of the notice to creditors. Then, for any known creditors, the personal representative needs to mail out something called a Notice to Creditors that informs them they have four months to present a claim. If they do not, then their claims are extinguished.

What If You Miss Someone Or Someone Contests the Probate?

What happens if someone is left out of the notification process or contests the will? That is when things get complicated. They essentially have a right to contest the process. Things may have sailed smoothly through the court system, and the personal representative is busy taking care of things. Then, suddenly, things can come to a screeching halt fast if someone files a petition with the court. They could contest the appointment or request an accounting. They could request supervised administration, for example, meaning that the court now has to get involved with approving all decisions. It can get complicated very quickly if someone is not properly notified.

In terms of contesting the will, that can also complicate things. A will can be contested for several reasons. One is undue influence. Suppose the person contesting believes that the deceased person was pressured somehow to sign the document. That can be a yearlong litigation track. They can contest it based on lack of capacity. They can question what the will says. We see this a lot of times in situations where the deceased person was trying to save some money, and maybe they went on the internet and got a form that is kind of ambiguous. Then, there may be a fight over what certain words mean and whether the personal representative has actual authority.

Contesting a Will

People will share horror stories they have heard about people contesting a will to intentionally slow down the process, so it takes years.

Do not worry about that. The courts in Arizona usually do not allow that. But I have seen situations in which a will contest or a dispute over a trust has gone on for years. What can happen is the court can make a determination, and one of the sides can appeal that, and the appeal takes six months. Then it goes back to the trial court, and the trial court must redo that decision, and maybe that decision or something else gets appealed. During the whole time, depositions and paperwork go back and forth, asking for information and documents, and it can be frustrating for everyone involved.

Key Point to Remember About Contacting People

Make sure you know who you need to notify. We are handling an estate for a lady who was not married and had no children. Her heirs numbered maybe 15 people at different levels of familial relation. In her case, there are several cousins, like a cousin who was once removed and a cousin who was twice removed. The strange thing is that our client is the personal representative, but she is a more distant cousin who, ironically, does not qualify as an heir. She was the one person who stayed in contact with the deceased person, but legally, she was not closely related enough to qualify as an heir.

She is handling the whole probate. One good thing is she can get paid hourly for her time, but she would rather sit and watch TV than do all this work for almost no reward. In the end, the money is going to end up going to a bunch of people who never knew the deceased person.

It took a long time to figure out who the heirs were, and we had to work closely with a genealogy company to do that.

Essential Takeaway:
Follow Arizona law strictly in notifying heirs, beneficiaries, and creditors.

Adhere to specific timelines and methods of notification. Document all notifications thoroughly as proof of compliance, and be aware that failure to properly notify can lead to legal challenges.

Chapter Four

Inventory and Appraisement of the Estate's Assets

How Do You Locate the Decedent's Accounts and Property?

Locating a deceased person's accounts and property, if you do not know where they are, can definitely be tricky. I came up with eight-pointers to help with that process.

1. Review personal documents. Look through the deceased person's files, such as previous tax returns, bank statements, and financial documents.

2. You can check the deceased person's mail and email. The personal representative should, immediately after getting appointed, have the mail forwarded to where they can receive it. Then, they can monitor the mail and look for account statements or correspondence from financial institutions.

3. Search for digital traces. See if you can access the deceased person's digital devices or accounts and look for digital records of accounts or assets. Maybe look for emails with monthly statements from a bank, for example.

4. Contact financial institutions. We sometimes ran into a situation where we had no idea where the bank was. My best advice was to start calling banks because there is a limited number of banks. I mean, in all likelihood, most people use a national bank, or there might be a credit union close by or something like that. Just start calling.

5. If you happen to know who the financial advisor or accountant was, you can talk to that person.

6. You can check the unclaimed property databases; there might be some information there.

7. Simply search for public records of ownership. For example, here in Maricopa County, you can enter the person's name on the Maricopa County

Assessor's website and see if there is any real estate owned by that person.

8. Look for a key to a safe deposit box. These have a distinctive shape that differs from a house or car key. With the Letters of Personal Representative, the person has the authority to contact banks and ask them to give access to the safe deposit box.

Will I Need Professional Appraisals Done?

Typically, we do not do professional appraisals because, for most people, the assets are personal property of nominal value, bank accounts and real estate. Old furniture and dishes aren't worth appraising. If there is valuable jewelry, you can have a jeweler give an appraisal. You can determine what a bank account is worth by looking at a bank statement. Then, if there is a house, you can figure out what that is worth because, if it ends up being sold, it is usually sold within a reasonable time after the person dies. That is a good assessment of what the value is. Otherwise, a real estate agent's market analysis of real estate is usually sufficient.

We do end up getting appraisals sometimes. If it is a more complicated situation or if the person is wealthier, maybe we have to think about estate taxes, for example. Another situation might be if one of the family members wants to buy the house. Then, we have to get an appraisal and do the calculation to figure out how much they should pay for the house to pay off the other beneficiaries, for example.

Preparing the Inventory and Appraisement

I am often asked if there are timelines or deadlines for getting professional appraisals. The personal representative has 90 days from when they are appointed to provide an "Inventory and Appraisement" to the heirs or interested persons. The inventory is supposed to list the different assets. I am not sure why they call it appraisement and not appraisal. I think appraisement is a fancy word for saying what you reckon the assets are worth and then providing that to the other side. It does not necessarily have to be done with professional appraisals.

There is a difference between market value and sentimental value. Families often get this confused. The court system is more concerned with market value. But sentimental value is what often fuels probate disputes.

We get situations like that a lot. For example, I had a situation about 20 years ago in which a father died and had a Rolex watch. Two of the sons each spent about $20,000 in legal fees fighting over this Rolex watch. It was only worth about $5,000, but it had such sentimental value that they both insisted on getting the watch.

In these situations, it is easy to confuse emotional value with monetary value. Always remember, once the emotions get involved, that means more money spent.

What Assets Tend to Be Overlooked on the Inventory?

Here's the thing about the inventory. The Arizona statute does not define what inventory means. Different people can have different ideas about that, which can create real conflict in this area. For example, I might think that an inventory of personal property would be simply listing "Contents of the house" and saying "nominal value." Someone else might think, "Well, no. For inventory, you need to list the dishes and the sofa and the TV and the military medals and this and that, and list everything out in a lot of detail."

It is important to agree with the other people involved, with the other family members, about what they expect in terms of an inventory, and also give them a heads-up about what the cost might be if they want a detailed inventory.

For example, I am dealing with a probate right now in which the deceased parents were collectors. You could say they were high-end hoarders. They had collectible dolls and porcelain figurines. During the process of doing the inventory, my client discovered that the dolls had mites in their hair. They ended up having to go through and pick out the nits or the little bugs from the dolls' hairs to be able to sell them. Then, she hired a professional inventory and estate management company to list and sell everything.

I am kind of making the numbers up here, but roughly, the property ended up selling for about $60,000, and the cost of the estate management company was about $55,000. One of the other family members is complaining that she spent too much money doing the inventory and selling the property. Frankly, I do not know what else she could have done. The point is that this is one of those areas that can lead to fights if it is not handled properly.

Essential Takeaway:
Be thorough and objective

Accurate valuation of estate assets is crucial for fair distribution and for meeting tax obligations. Consider hiring professional appraisers for real estate, valuable personal property, and business interests.

Chapter Five
Payment of Debts and Taxes

How Do I Make Sure I Pay All Legitimate Debts, and What Happens If I Miss Some?

We covered this a little bit earlier, but to ensure that the legitimate debts of an estate are paid, the personal representative in Arizona needs to follow certain steps. The first step is to publish a notice to creditors in a local newspaper, like we talked about before. That notice gets published once a week for three consecutive weeks. It announces the appointment of the personal representative, the person's address, and instructions for creditors to present their claims within four months of the first publication of the notice. Then, as I mentioned before, you also mail a notice to known creditors that tells them that they have a certain amount of time to present their claims.

Reviewing and Addressing Claims

The personal representative should review claims submitted by the creditors and decide if they are valid or not. Then they have to decide whether to pay them. The Arizona statutes are unforgiving in terms of the deadline. If a creditor misses a deadline, then they are out of luck. Conversely, if a personal representative fails to deny a claim within a specific deadline, they can be out of luck. And the personal representative could be held personally liable for the mistake, as I'll explain now.

I had a situation several years ago in which the personal representative should have denied a claim filed by the ex-husband. Because she did not, she went through a year of litigation over a stupid claim, and she ended up running up legal fees because of this. If the personal representative had simply met the deadline and denied the claim within the required time, that could have all been prevented. As a result, the personal representative was personally responsible for the legal fees that could have been prevented. This is not an area to be played around with.

What Taxes Is the Estate Responsible For? What Happens If Debts and Taxes Are More Than the Estate Assets?

The relevant taxes can include any remaining income taxes the deceased person might have owed. Also, for a larger estate, there might be federal estate taxes. Whether there are estate taxes depends on the year because the amount fluctuates, but I will just generally say this is a concern for a much larger estate.

What happens if debts and taxes are more than assets? There is a statute that says what happens. Debts are required to be paid in a specific order. By the way, debts have to get paid before the beneficiaries or the heirs get anything.

First, the costs and expenses of administration are paid. Those are expenses incurred in administering the estate, such as court fees, legal fees, and compensation of the personal representative's time. Next in line are reasonable funeral expenses. Debts and taxes with preference under federal law are next. This includes the IRS. Next are the medical and hospital expenses of the last illness. After that comes state taxes or other expenses with preference under the state law. After that are all other claims like credit cards, for example.

You just kind of do it like a waterfall and go down the list. Let's say you only have enough to cover the costs and expenses of administration, and there is not even enough to cover all of that. Then, you just do the math to determine how much the estate can pay. Perhaps you can only pay 80% of the legal fees and 80% of the fees of the personal representative and other administrative costs, and then it stops there. You just go down the line until there is no money left.

My Encouragement to You

It is easy to get trigger-happy when it comes to paying debts and taxes. It is easy to just pay a bill as it comes in. I would encourage you to just hold off and get through the creditor waiting period of four months. That way, you know exactly who the creditors are, what the debts are, what the taxes are, and then decide who gets paid and so on. Otherwise, let's say you pay a $20,000 credit card and then pay off the home mortgage, and then suddenly, the IRS comes up with a tax lien, and there is not enough money to cover that. You could be held personally liable if you paid other debts with lower priority.

I would encourage you to just be methodical and get a lawyer involved. I mean, this is one of those things you can be personally liable if you make the wrong choice.

Sometimes Being in a Rush Gets Expensive.

Let's say the loved one had only credit card bills, their house was paid off, and they lived very frugally. Does the family still need to wait four months to pay the credit card bills, or can they go ahead and pay those things as they come in?

As a lawyer, I would say to be more conservative. You may know exactly what the situation was. If you were close to your loved one, you may already have a pretty good sense of what there is. If there is a $500,000 house and a $1,000 credit card, you may be able to make a judgment call about paying off the credit card. My advice, though, would always be to do things methodically. I have learned over the past 25 years that you cannot predict what is going to happen.

Essential Takeaway:
Prioritize debts and taxes before distributing assets to beneficiaries.

Understand the order of priority for debts as per Arizona law and ensure that all tax obligations, both federal and state, are met. Keep detailed records of all payments.

Chapter Six
Final Accounting

The final accounting includes the list of assets you began with and debts and expenses that were paid. Then, you list income or gains that the estate assets have generated during the administration process, such as interest dividends or profits from the sale of assets. If there have been any partial distributions to beneficiaries, you then list those. After that, you have a balance of remaining assets. You subtract fees for the personal representative and fees for professionals such as a lawyer or a CPA. Finally, you come up with a balance remaining for distribution. That is what the final accounting means.

How Do Beneficiaries Get Their Inheritance?

After the debts, taxes and administration expenses have been paid, you can start thinking about distributing funds to the beneficiaries. The timeline can vary depending on the complexity of the estate and the probate process. In some cases, partial distributions may have already been made, but final distributions usually occur after the final accounting gets approved. Now you have a judgment call about how to make sure you can make a distribution and consider everything done.

The last thing you want to do as a personal representative is to give a bunch of money to all the heirs, only to have them use that money to hire attorneys and fight with you. You want to have some finality here. One of the things we do is what is called a Proposal for Distribution. This is permitted by statute. You can provide an accounting to the heirs, and it can be informal. It might be just copies of bank statements, giving people a sense of what there was, what the expenses were, and what was left over. The proposal says, "Here is what you are all going to get." Under the statute, they have 30 days to object to that. If the heirs do not object, then you are good. Then, under the statute, they are deemed to have waived their right to object, and you can distribute it safely.

When Do the Beneficiaries Get Paid?

As far as the timing for people to get their inheritance, I would say the earliest would be six months after the deceased person died. That is because you should wait for the creditor period to expire, so that is four months. You probably have to sell some things and do some other work. After that, you have to send out a Proposal for Distribution and wait for 30 days. If everyone is working super-fast, the earliest that is going to happen is six months from the date of death.

Now, if someone questions the numbers or doesn't agree with the Proposal for Distribution, their option is to request that the court review the accounting. They might also request a supervised administration. Those are two different things. Let's talk about the petition for an accounting first. They want the court to review things. What is probably going to happen then is the accounting is going to be submitted to the court accountant's office. Here in Maricopa County, that office currently has around an eight-month delay or backlog in terms of just being able to look at accountings.

If you do not want to delay the whole process, you have to be careful how you present this to the court. Essentially, everyone would be given notice of the hearing, and then there would ultimately be an evidentiary hearing. During this, the judge or the probate commissioner would make a determination on what improprieties went on or whether the personal representative made some mistakes. But realistically, that could be a year later. So, it's generally better to look for other ways of resolving disputes over the numbers.

Essential Takeaway:
Maintain transparency and accuracy.

The final accounting should provide a clear and detailed report of all income, expenses, debts paid, and distributions made from the estate. This document is critical for closing the estate and should be prepared with meticulous attention to detail.

Chapter Seven
Closing of the Estate

Closing the estate means you are notifying the court that you have completed the administration. It could also be a way of releasing yourself from further liability or responsibility for how you handled the estate as a personal representative. There are two different ways to do this.

For most situations, you can close the estate informally, and that just means filing a Closing Statement with the court. That statement indicates that the personal representative has completed all the necessary tasks, such as paying debts and taxes, distributing the remaining assets to the rightful beneficiaries, and providing a final account of their administration. That simply gets filed, and that is it. There is no hearing or anything else.

The benefit of doing an informal closing is it is cheaper and quicker. However, the downside is that you do not get a court order saying that you are formally discharged. The other way of doing this is by closing the estate formally with a court hearing.

You would file a petition with the court to resolve any dispute if there was infighting in the family. Some examples of problematic situations include fighting over what happened, allegations of mismanagement, or if the personal representative took too long or made bad decisions.

This may or may not be tied in with the accounting. The personal representative might file what is called a Petition for Approval of Final Accounting and for a Decree of Settlement and Distribution of the Estate. If they are asking for an accounting, that goes through the court accountant's office. As such, there is going to be a many-month delay in that whole process. The way it is typically done with a formal closing is by submitting the accounting and the request to be formally discharged.

The benefit of doing it that way would be you would have an actual court order saying that you are good. You would then know that family members cannot come back later and sue you for something, but it is more complicated. Usually, instead of asking for a formal supervised closing process, we can work with family members and try to provide them with the information they want and then send the Proposal for Distribution, as I talked about before. In 99% of cases, that is sufficient.

Why Do You Need an Attorney at this Point?

It is important to have an attorney with you because some parts of probate can be done informally, but some parts need to be done formally to protect the representative. If you try to do everything informally, you may not have the same protections as you would with an attorney helping you. We would be able to guide you in different ways to save not only money but also time and grief.

What Is a Formal Discharge?

Formal discharge is a legal process that officially concludes the personal representative's duties and responsibilities in administering a deceased person's estate. This discharge typically occurs after the personal representative has completed all tasks related to the estate, such as paying debts, distributing assets to beneficiaries, and filing necessary tax returns. The court, upon reviewing and approving the final accounting and activities of the estate, issues an order of discharge, releasing the personal representative from further obligations and liability related to the estate. This formal discharge provides legal closure to the administration of the estate.

Why Would You Want to Get Formally Discharged as a Personal Representative?

The first reason you would want a formal discharge is that it provides official legal closure and confirms that the personal representative has fulfilled all of their duties and obligations. Reason number two for seeking formal discharge would be protection from future claims. It can protect the personal representative from future claims or liabilities related to their role in administering the estate. Number three is that it provides clarity for beneficiaries and heirs. It clarifies to the beneficiaries, heirs, and creditors that the estate has been fully settled and closed. Number four, it can provide a way of resolving disputes in cases in which there have been disputes among beneficiaries. For example, a formal discharge can serve as an official way of resolving those disputes.

How do you do it? As I mentioned before, you file a petition with the court for an order of complete settlement. That is also accompanied by a petition to approve the accounting. That is the way it is done in Arizona. It would be a Petition to Approve Accounting and for a Decree of Settlement and Distribution of the Estate. Then, you have to provide notice to the interested parties. There has to be a court hearing. After the hearing, if the court is satisfied, the personal representative gets formally discharged.

Essential Takeaway:
Ensure all steps have been completed.

This includes paying all debts and taxes, distributing all assets, and providing interested parties with the final accounting (or getting them to sign a Waiver of Final Accounting). Obtain receipts from beneficiaries for distributed assets. If appropriate, file a petition with the court to close the estate. Ensure you have something in writing that releases you from further responsibility.

Chapter Eight
Importance of Hiring an Attorney

Serving as a personal representative of an estate in Arizona can be a complex and demanding role. Without the guidance of a probate lawyer, personal representatives may inadvertently make mistakes that could have serious consequences. Here are some common errors to be aware of.

Number one is just misunderstanding the law. As you can probably tell if you have gotten this far in the book, probate and estate laws can be complex, and they can vary from state to state. If you are from a different state, you might think you know how probate goes, but it can be completely different here in Arizona. Misinterpreting the laws can result in legal missteps. For example, failing to understand the specific rules for notice to creditors or proper order of debt repayment can lead to legal issues.

Number two is improper asset management, and I see this a lot, unfortunately. A personal representative is responsible for managing the estate's assets until they are distributed. This can include securing property, managing investments, and maintaining or selling real estate. A mistake I sometimes see is mixing personal funds with estate funds or misusing estate assets. That can lead to allegations of embezzlement or breach of fiduciary duty. Without proper legal guidance, there is a risk of mismanaging the assets and potentially leading to losses for the estate and beneficiaries.

Number three would be the failure to properly notify creditors and beneficiaries. The estate's personal representative has to notify creditors and beneficiaries in the manner prescribed by law, and failure to do so correctly can result in claims against the estate or disputes among beneficiaries.

Number four is the improper distribution of assets. Distributing assets to beneficiaries before all debts and taxes have been settled can result in personal financial liability for the personal representative.

Number five is the lack of record-keeping. Inadequate record-keeping of financial transactions and decisions can lead to disputes and legal challenges.

Six is missing deadlines. There are specific timelines for filing documents and completing various probate tasks. Missing these deadlines can delay the process and potentially lead to penalties.

Seven is inadequate communication with beneficiaries. Poor communication can lead to misunderstandings, disputes, and potential litigation.

Eight is ignoring family disputes. Not addressing or mediating disputes among beneficiaries can escalate conflicts, leading to legal battles and draining estate resources.

Another mistake, and we talked about this earlier, is failing to close the estate properly. Not completing all the necessary steps to formally close the probate process can leave the estate in legal limbo.

I could keep going.

When Is Legal Advice Critical?

I would say that, ideally, there should be a probate attorney involved from the very beginning. Legal advice at the start can help you understand the legal process, your role, and what needs to happen. This will save time and avoid complications from doing things incorrectly.

Also, if there are disputes or claims among beneficiaries or claims by creditors, that would be a point to get a probate attorney involved. You, as the personal representative, can be personally liable for making the wrong decision. You are now potentially involved in litigation, and that is governed by the civil rules of procedure. There are also probate rules and statutes, and there is also case law. As a probate attorney, it is hard for me to keep up with everything. If it is complicated for me, it is dangerous for someone trying to figure out what to do without having an attorney involved.

I recently had a client ask how hiring an attorney could help save time, money, and headaches during probate. I told them, "An attorney acts as a guide, simplifying the probate process and providing peace of mind during a challenging time. By entrusting these legal complexities to a professional, you can focus on grieving and healing, knowing that your loved one's estate is being managed with care and expertise."

GENERAL FIDUCIARY
DUTIES OF
PERSONAL REPRESENTATIVE

- Duty of fairness and impartiality to the beneficiaries and the creditors of the Estate.

- Duty to be cautious and prudent in dealing with Estate assets.

- Duty to never use estate assets for your personal benefit or mix them with your assets or anyone else's assets.

- Duty to avoid a conflict of interest between the personal representative's fiduciary obligations and the personal representative's individual interests.

- Duty to not profit from dealing with Estate assets, other than receiving reasonable compensation for your services as personal representative.

- Duty to comply with the Order to Personal Representative.

Chapter Nine
Probate Myths to Avoid

When handling a probate, it's crucial to be aware of common myths and misunderstandings that can lead to mistakes or mismanagement. Here are three key probate myths that seem to be out there.

The first myth is that an executor or personal representative can distribute assets immediately. But in reality, assets should not be distributed until all debts, taxes, and administrative expenses of the estate have been paid. If you distribute the estate prematurely, you could be personally on the hook if you later discover a debt and there isn't enough left over to pay it.

Another myth is that probate just involves distributing assets according to the will. While distributing assets according to the will is a significant part of probate, it's not the only responsibility. The personal representative must also identify and gather all the decedent's assets, pay debts and taxes, manage the property until distribution, maintain accurate records, and sometimes file final personal and estate tax returns. There may be questions involving the interpretation of the will. It's a comprehensive process that involves more than just following the directives of the will.

Third, there is a common perception that the court system should be avoided at all costs. So, if there's a dispute, it's best to either ignore it or try to handle it informally. Unfortunately, that's sometimes not practical. While amicable resolution is ideal, disputes can be complex and legally challenging. If a dispute can't be resolved informally, it's best to get the court involved sooner rather than later. This ensures that the resolution is legally sound and protects the personal representative from future claims of mismanagement or bias.

I had a case recently where a house was partly owned by the deceased parent. An adult child of the decedent continued to live in the house. The personal representative, another adult child, waited years before deciding to take court action to evict the sibling from the house and be able to sell it. By that time, the whole situation had become very complicated and blew up into messy probate litigation.

For anyone handling a probate, understanding these realities is vital to avoid common pitfalls. It's important to recognize when to seek professional advice, especially in complex situations or when facing legal uncertainties.

My Hope for You

I hope that, through this book, I have shed at least some light on the probate process so that you have a clearer and more comprehensive understanding. Hopefully, you also feel more empowered with the ability to navigate the probate process confidently. I also hope that I have highlighted the potential risks involved with trying to go it alone because it is easy to make mistakes. Whether it is our law firm or someone else, it is important to have an experienced probate law firm to guide you through the process and help you avoid pitfalls.

What You Think Should Happen May Not Be Legal

There is a difference between what you think should happen and what the law says. For example, your deceased loved one may have said, "Make sure you do this and that, and someone is supposed to get this item. This is what I want to happen with the house and everything." If legal documents say something other than that, or if there are no legal documents, then you must follow the law. You can be held accountable for trying to carry out informal verbal statements that are not supported by the law.

You have to make sure you know what you are supposed to do. Unfortunately, a lot of people do informal planning. One of the problems with that is they may have told one relative that this is supposed to happen and then told another relative something else is supposed to happen. When the person dies, those two relatives fight with each other over what they think is supposed to happen. And despite their fighting, the law may say something completely different. It is good to just get someone involved to make sure things go smoothly.

Chapter Ten
Here's How We Can Help You

What Happens in Our Initial Meeting?

In our first meeting, I will try to understand your needs as the client. The meeting begins with me listening to your situation, hearing about your role, and the specific challenges you are facing. Then, I review relevant details. That might involve reviewing documents like wills and other documents. I will then summarize those and give a legal explanation and legal guidance. Based on the information that you provided, I explain the relevant legal concepts and procedures, hopefully clearly and without legal jargon, so you understand.

Then, I provide tailored legal advice. Offering advice tailored to the specific situation considers factors like the size of the estate, the types of assets, the potential for disputes and other state-specific laws. At the end, we will discuss potential strategies and the next steps to manage the probate process efficiently and effectively.

How You Can Contact Me

Call me directly at **(602) 904-7943**, or go online to **www.ProbateMadeSimple.com.**

Simplifying the Probate Process

After losing a loved one, not only are you working through your grief, but you also need to navigate the probate process. Complex legal procedures can often feel overwhelming and can even create family conflicts and delays. At the same time, doing probate incorrectly can end up creating unnecessary expenses and confusion.

Probate does not have to be a burden. My goal with this book is to guide you through probate with not only 25 years of experience but also with compassion.

You will learn how to handle every step smoothly, from filing petitions to distributing inheritances, while minimizing costs and family tensions. My wish is to empower you to settle estates efficiently, regardless of size or complexity, so you can honor legacies, care for your family, and move forward with peace of mind.

To learn more about the ideas discussed in this book, here is what you do next.

Go to **www.ProbateMadeSimple.com** to

Step 1: Download the **3 Missteps Out of State Personal Representatives Often Make** and how to avoid them.

Step 2: Download the **Probate Terminology Worksheet** to familiarize yourself with all the legal documents you will need.

Step 3: Grab a **Brainstorm Call** to see if you are better prepared to handle probate than you thought.

Made in the USA
Columbia, SC
31 July 2024